WHEN THE SUN SLEEPS

A Pride and Prejudice Novella

ALIX JAMES

NICOLE CLARKSTON

Copyright © 2020 by Alix James

All rights reserved.

Cover art by Natterarts

No part of this book may be reproduced in any form or by any electronic or mechanical means, including information storage and retrieval systems, without written permission from the author, except for the use of brief quotations in a book review.

For my husband
The reason I keep dreaming

CHAPTER 1

Of all this, she might have been mistress.

Elizabeth gazed in awe out of the carriage window at the sweeping majesty of Pemberley. The house—a noble structure if ever she had seen one—stood on a moderate prominence, flanked in the rear by a rising wood and surrounded on the fore with a natural scape, rather than the rigid formal gardens of many other estates. Rolling out from a hill to the east was a low stream, swelled in the midst of the clearing by the hand of man, yet so tastefully done that the surroundings would scarce have been complete without the bulrushes and lilies that graced its banks.

"If you like the prospect from here, Lizzy, the house itself is ten times grander," her Aunt Gardiner promised.

"I confess I am eager to see it," her uncle agreed, "though taking the full tour of Pemberley means we will not make Ambergate by nightfall."

"Oh, let us not," Elizabeth protested. "Truly, I have no interest in fine houses and such splendors. Let us continue with our original plan, shall we?"

Mrs. Gardiner looked crestfallen. "I thought you should like to see the home of a man whose acquaintance you claimed. We have the whole month to explore the Peaks."

"But what is Mr. Darcy to me? Surely, it would be a pointless venture."

"I thought he was a great friend of Mr. Bingley. Was I mistaken? And as the other gentleman is lately returned to Hertfordshire and has proved his remorse and loyalty to Jane in such a pretty fashion, I should think Mr. Darcy might occasionally enter your circle."

"Mr. Bingley says that Mr. Darcy has sworn off all his acquaintances, though he would not say why. Truly, Aunt, it would be most impolitic for us to impose upon his solitude."

"Guests do not tour the family's private rooms, Lizzy," her uncle scoffed. "And it is not likely he would be there, in any case."

Elizabeth allowed her eyes to rest longingly on the home that belonged to the man whose heart she had broken—the home that might have been hers, had she only been more cautious in her allegiances and more temperate with her words.

"Please, let us drive on. You said we might stop at Chatsworth tomorrow, and is that house not almost twice as grand?"

"But not half so well suited to *your* tastes," Mrs. Gardiner relented in a wounded tone.

"Then, as you are quite determined that I should like Pemberley above all others," Elizabeth suggested, "perhaps we may defer that tour until we stop at Lambton on our return journey. Surely, your friends there will gladly give us a tour."

"Very well." Mr. Gardiner rapped on the roof of the carriage. "Drive on, John."

Elizabeth refused to look over her shoulder as they turned about, but it was no use. Pemberley—its grounds, the house, and the visage of its master—were as clear in her eye as if she had never looked away.

<hr />

"You wished to see me, sir?"

Darcy turned from the window as Mrs. Reynolds entered his study. "I did not mean to disturb you. I heard someone else desired a tour of the house?"

"Yes, sir. A most agreeable family from London. They were quite disappointed, for they had heard such praises of the portrait gallery, but they were very sympathetic when they learned why the house was closed."

Darcy nodded. He never went to the portrait gallery anymore. Instead of speaking what he would rather not, or watching the tragic way dear Mrs. Reynolds tried not to dab at her eyes when she mentioned the gallery, he looked out the window again. A carriage was leaving the main drive, and a second could be seen in the distance—but it was turning around without ever approaching the house. That was well—poor Mrs. Reynolds would be spared sending them away.

"Mrs. Reynolds, I want you to close up the house."

She was silent until he looked back at her, and he found her blinking in awe. "More so than it already is, sir?"

"Not merely for tours. I would have all of it closed down. I am going to Scotland for a time. Shroud it all, cover the paintings, and turn anyone away who even wishes to see the gardens. They may walk the paths by the lake, I suppose—a trifling consolation for coming all this way, but there are other houses to tour. Houses that do not boast of grief more than grandeur."

She was slightly pale, and for a moment, Darcy regretted the monstrous thing he had asked of her. She delighted in showing off his home; it was her pride and the last joy of her heart. Everyone at Pemberley took enormous pride in the beauty of their home, even down to the lad who helped the gardener weed the rose beds.

But without Georgiana... without any survivors of the Darcy line but himself... it was a hollow vanity to subject these halls to pleasure tours.

"I will see it done, sir," she said, in as steady a voice as he had ever heard her employ. Her lashes, however, were damp.

"I have spoken with my steward. What matters are not directly his to oversee will be within your jurisdiction. I have faith you will both manage better than I while I am away."

Mrs. Reynolds' chin quivered, but she gave a resolute nod. "Sir."

"It is only for the season," he soothed. "No doubt I will come to my senses ere long and do my part. I've no intention of letting the reputation of the house suffer for my bitterness."

"It is not the house for which I weep, sir, but yourself."

He sighed and came near to the woman who had nearly replaced his mother in the measure of maternal affections. "No sense weeping for me, Mrs. Reynolds. I am afraid I am a lost cause."

She spoke some loyal platitude, then went away soon after. Darcy leaned heavily on the casement, trying to keep his eyes from blurring. Today marked one year from the day his world had started to crumble, and three months from the day his universe had died altogether. What remained but exile and seclusion for him?

No, he did not feel selfish in wanting to secure Pemberley as a mausoleum. Nor did he feel unjustified in his course. He meant to go to Scotland... and probably never come back.

CHAPTER 2

Chatsworth was, indeed, a marvel to the senses, but for Elizabeth, it did nothing to inspire the soul. Perhaps that was why her aunt had so desired to show her Pemberley. Even admiring that house from a distance for a few seconds had set free some fluttering creature in her breast. She could have wandered there for hours, if given leave, and have only felt the more at home with each new scene. Chatsworth was everything awe-inspiring and splendid, but it did not whisper to her long after her eyes had closed in sleep.

They stayed in Bakewell for two nights, and then her aunt proposed going on to Ferndale. She had old friends there and desired to remain above a week in the area. "For Lizzy could climb the rocks to her heart's content by day, and by evening, we could be in very comfortable company," she said.

Mr. Gardiner and Elizabeth were agreeable, so to Ferndale they went on the third day. Elizabeth had a letter from home, penned in Jane's quaking hand, in which the latter announced Mr. Bingley's continued attentions, and the hopes raging wildly through Longbourn. *This* time, everyone said, Mr. Bingley was sure to come to the point, for there was no Miss Bingley and no Mr. Darcy to disapprove.

Elizabeth had wondered on more than one occasion if Mr. Darcy was not rather the reason Mr. Bingley had hastened to Hertfordshire earlier in the summer, but she dared not speak of her suspicions. It was enough for her that Jane was happy. There was a segment of the letter, however, that made the chill race to Elizabeth's bones.

Lizzy, there is something terribly distressing I must now relate to you. It comes from Lydia, in Brighton. She reports that our once and former friend, Mr. Wickham, has been killed. The rumor is that it was an illegal duel, but she cannot learn more about the circumstances or the offense that engendered the challenge.

For my part, I am sorry. I recall what you told me of his character, but I had dearly hoped he might have reformed. I fear this sad event is indicative that he did not—or, perhaps, that past deeds found him out. I should like to think him innocent, but I am afraid even I cannot find him guiltless with so much evidence to the contrary.

Elizabeth stopped reading to gaze at the fire. *Mr. Wickham dead?* There was remorse in this discovery, it was true, but overriding it a tremendous sense of guilt. Mr. Wickham had made an art of deceit, and at one time, she had been among his most eager patrons. How many had been harmed through her own actions? Was he killed by the offended father of some other young woman he had attempted to seduce? Though she could not make herself culpable, she regretted not speaking clearer warnings before it was too late. A bit of caution from her might have even protected Mr. Wickham from such an end.

She sighed and kept reading. Jane's letter went on to describe the doings of their young cousins. Elizabeth chucked especially over the part about how little Tommy had persuaded Mr. Bingley to give him a pointer puppy—all to please Jane, no doubt, until the puppy chewed her best slippers.

Elizabeth folded the letter thoughtfully. She would pen her reply on the morrow, after some reflection, and once she knew the address of their next lodgings. She had much she longed to say to her sister.

※

Darcy could not stop thinking of her. Occasionally, he would look out the window just so, and a phantom would pass by, bearing her image. The dark eyes would laugh, her light figure would twirl about his vision, and some unheard remark would coax an almost-smile from him—he, who had stopped smiling forever in April.

He thought he saw her again last night—at an inn in Bakewell, of all places. A young lady with the same figure had entered the inn while he was still across the street at the ostler. She never turned around, but there was no need for him to see her face to know it was not her. Elizabeth Bennet has no business in Derbyshire—in fact, would probably avoid it at all costs.

Just as well. He had nothing left to offer one so full of joy, even if their paths were to cross again. In fact, it was possible she lived in dread of such an event, especially after

Bingley had taken his advice and returned to Hertfordshire. She might expect to see him, as well. That was one thing, at least, he could do for her—spare her such mortification, and stay entirely away.

He had not brought his carriage on this journey. He preferred rather to remain at liberty, for once in his life, to come and go as he pleased, with no one the wiser about his location. A bag behind his saddle served as his valet, and his horse his only company. He would not inflict his abysmal spirits on anyone.

And he was in no hurry. What he proposed... it was more than he could engage for at present. Therefore, he took the less-traveled roads, the quaint scenic inns. Perhaps a day or two taking in the sights along the way might not go amiss, as he bent his path on that northern road.

He had no notion of where he was going, really. He only meant to become a no one bound for nowhere. When he came to a crossroads late in the day, with signposts announcing two towns, both three miles distant, he let his horse make the choice. Ferndale it was. Darcy had never stayed in that town, but so long as it boasted a bed, it would be good enough.

"I am sorry, sir, but the top floor was taken only an hour ago," the innkeeper apologized.

"No, no, you mistake me," Darcy answered wearily. "I am traveling alone. I do not wish for an entire floor. I ask only a quiet room."

The innkeeper held a brief conference with his wife, then cleared his throat. "Being as you are a gentleman of quality, I think I can still offer you one of our best rooms. The other party did not take the entire floor—only two rooms and the sitting room adjoining the suites. There is another, though the window faces full west. It is a good family next door, quiet and respectable. I am sorry, it is the best I have."

"It will suffice," Darcy grunted. "I will be dining in my room, please."

CHAPTER 3

The dining in the common room was exceptionally good. Elizabeth particularly enjoyed the warm crusty bread served with her soup, and went to her room feeling contented and mellow. Mr. and Mrs. Gardiner retired to their bedchamber directly, her aunt claiming a faint headache. Elizabeth, however, decided to write back to Jane.

They had reserved the sitting room that connected to her bedroom, and there was a secretary in the corner in which she found ink and paper for her purpose. Elizabeth stoked the fire and set happily to work. Jane must be informed of all the sights they had passed, the people they had met, and the wonders of the magnificent houses they had toured. She left out the house they did not tour.

By the time she was finished, her mind was too alive with its own ideas and uncomfortable notions for sleep. She had brought a book, which she had already read so many times she could recite it. Though she was no dedicated seamstress, her embroidery seemed the most promising outlet for her restlessness. She settled in a wooden rocker and pushed off with her toes, setting the old chair creaking in time to her stitches, and began to hum.

***

Darcy lay awake, staring at the ceiling. He had scarcely bothered to undress, and was still clad in his breeches and tail shirt. His dinner, what remained of it, still stood in the corner on a tray, for he had asked the maid to leave it. Not that it mattered how long the bread and cold tea stood there, nor how his stomach rumbled. None of it held any flavor.

He had always accounted himself a man who had everything to live for. It was true—a full measure and a half of life's usual blessings had been poured over him by nature of birth, and even more had fallen his way through the course of his years. Even with the weight of all the Darcy name and duties falling his way while he was yet a young man mourning his parents, he had not been insensible to the many gifts granted him.

Yet, the delights dearest to his heart had all been swept away in almost a moment, and what remained... vast and extravagant as it was... was nothing to what he had lost.

It was wrong to cast himself away like this. Whether he simply vanished from all memory like a vagrant son, or whether he found a peaceful end to his pain, nothing could absolve him of the guilt of disappointing those who still depended on him. But what was life to him now but an ever-present reminder of his many failings?

As he ruminated in the darkness, a faint sound seemed to answer his question. A creak, low and regular, echoed under the far door. Darcy sat up.

The door led to a sitting room, the innkeeper had said, reserved by that family he had spoken of. There were locks

WHEN THE SUN SLEEPS

on each side of the door, so the rooms could be secured for different parties, or opened as needed. And just now, someone else was there, awake.

Darcy lay back, determined to ignore his neighbor, but the gentle thump and squeak of the chair pulsed in time to his heartbeat. And something else... a song. A horribly familiar one. He sat up again.

It was a woman's voice, humming softly in tempo with her toes against the floorboards. It was a pleasant, homey sounding voice—a tone like a mother's for her babe, or a maiden pining for her true love. Without knowing precisely why, he ached to hear it better.

He tiptoed to the door and listened. The voice broke for a moment, and Darcy was almost disappointed, thinking the woman had drifted to sleep or gone to bed. But then, the tune picked up where it had left off, and Darcy could only squeeze his eyes as the tears leaked out.

His mother used to hum that song to him. And Georgiana used to play it. And one time—only once—Elizabeth Bennet had sung it, in a rich and full-bodied voice that still haunted him. He bit his lip to restrain a gasp and rested his head on the door.

The latch rattled.

Darcy stiffened, and heard a shuffling of feet on the far side. "Is someone there?" whispered the lady.

Fool. Blasted idiot, mooning like a calf over some stranger's humming. Now she would think her neighbor to be a disreputable cad, troubling her at night! He cleared his throat and spoke in the lowest tones he could manage. No sense in alarming anyone else.

"Forgive me, madam. I did not mean to disturb you."

He heard her feet crossing to the door. "It is I who should beg forgiveness. I did not know anyone was in that room. I will leave you in peace and not keep you awake."

"Pray—" he almost begged—"do not assume your humming troubled me. Quite the opposite, in fact. I was already restless and it... has been a long while since I heard that song."

She was quiet for a moment. "Are you also having trouble sleeping?"

He grunted silently. "I have not slept in months."

"Months! Pray, sir, how are you still alive?"

Despite himself, he almost chuckled at the light jest in her tone. "I meant it figuratively."

"Then you must find something to occupy yourself. I was up writing a letter to my sister."

Darcy closed his eyes. "I have no sister to write to."

There was a second of silence beyond the door, then —"Well, after I sealed my letter, I began work on my embroidery. I have extra needles and thread, and would happily push them under the door if you would like to amuse yourself. How is your French Knot or your pistil stitch?"

"I am afraid I would be pricking the needle into my fingers more often than the fabric," he retorted with a half-smile.

"Oh, and we cannot have blood on the linens. What would the innkeeper think? He might even report you as either an invalid or a nuisance, and what then? Your travels would be dreadfully delayed."

Was that an honest grin, trying to fight its way across his face? Surely, there was something in his voice when he replied. "I have no precise schedule to keep. So long as I pay my bill, which I have done in advance, I doubt the innkeeper will mind overmuch if I damage the linens by my wounds."

"Oh, dear, that is even more troubling."

"Troubling?" he asked. "How so?"

"Why, do you see, if no one is expecting you, and you have paid your bill in advance, there will be no one to search for you and come to your aid after you maim yourself with a sewing needle. I suppose you will suffer for days, with no one the wiser, unless you can muster enough strength to crawl to the door and beseech some passer-by for help."

"Then," he answered, with his lips twitching oddly, "I must decline your very kind offer of the embroidery work. My health and safety would not withstand my ineptitude with such a sharp object."

"Perhaps you could perform some calisthenics to wear down your energy," she suggested. "Do not many gentlemen engage in such an activity to strengthen themselves?"

"Those who have strength to train, yes. What makes you think I am such a specimen?"

"Indeed, how very indelicate of me!" she cried. "And now I shall comfortably imagine you as a man of five and sixty, with graying hair and wizened cheeks, who depends upon his cane to walk and lies awake all night because he has dozed over his paper most of the day."

Darcy could not help it. He chuckled. For the first time in... well, since last April, a burst of amusement overtook him. "It would be unjust for me to permit such a portrait of myself, madam. No true gentleman could countenance a lady assuming he is... so harmless as that."

"Oh, you entice me with a mystery! It is most unfair, sir, for now, my mind will be tormented with all manner of imaginings, and I shall not rest. There is nothing else for it," she sighed. "You must sing to me."

He blinked. *What?* "Sing to you?"

"Indeed, for as you claimed the pleasure of hearing me humming when I did not know myself to have an audience,

I should like to indulge in hearing a gentleman crooning me to sleep. You *are* a gentleman, are you not?"

"I am."

"Then sing to me, if you please. We may both profit by the endeavor."

Sing to her? Insupportable! Why, never had he lifted his voice in song since he was a lad, and was not about to begin now, with a stranger in the dark. "I do not know any appropriate melodies," he offered lamely.

"You heard the one I was humming. Surely you are capable of repeating it. Come, do not resort to your dignity as an excuse. Who am I to speak to of your musical talents?"

He shook his head in wonder. The woman, whoever she was, was cunningly persistent. And something familiar in her tones—something that pulled on his heart like few other things could—made it impossible for him to refuse.

"I will hum to you," he relented, "on one condition. You must accompany me."

"Then we are agreed." He almost heard laughter in her voice, and he would have asked more about her that very instant, but immediately she settled into that poignant melody that split his ribs once more. Darcy gulped the hard lump in his throat and, tentatively, joined his deeper tones to her light ones.

Tears were streaming down his cheeks by the time the melody reached its end, but something had dislodged in his chest with that simple song. He released a long sigh and heard the woman's hand touching softly on the door.

"Good night, sir. Sleep well."

Darcy swallowed. "Good night, madam. And... thank you."

And for the first time in three months, Darcy slept.

CHAPTER 4

Elizabeth looked around the common room at breakfast, wondering at the identity of her midnight neighbor. She hesitated to inform her aunt of the odd conversation through the door, but her curiosity was powerful enough to continually turn her head.

That man there, with the green waistcoat. Perhaps he... no, he looked as though he spent more time smoking his pipe and drinking than lying awake at night.

Could it be that young man in the corner, with the bright red hair and the fair voice that laughed with the other travelers? Oh, no, impossible. The man next door had sounded more heartbroken than anyone Elizabeth had ever heard. Capable of amusement, to be sure, but underlying his light banter with her had been something fragile and unspoken. If he had only used his full voice, rather than hushed murmurs, she might know him when she met him face to face. Alas, it was not to be, and perhaps it was best.

They spent the day reacquainting themselves with Mrs. Gardiner's friends. Despite the allure of the mountains and rocks, Elizabeth was obliged to take tea and indulge children and provide an arm for her aunt's support when the ladies walked in the garden.

She was beginning to worry about her aunt. Mrs. Gardiner had begun this trip so hale and cheerful, but now she seemed frequently fatigued, occasionally out of breath, and often more sensitive than usual. Elizabeth had her own suspicions, but neither her aunt nor uncle had confirmed them for her, so she merely watched carefully over her aunt during the day, and let her uncle manage at night.

When they returned to the inn, it was quite late. Again, Aunt Gardiner retired at once, leaving Elizabeth to her amusements. She glanced at her book, frowned at her needlework, and decided that neither held her interest. Instead, she sat down with pen and paper again until she heard footsteps next door. Perhaps it was the same gentleman, or perhaps it was someone new. She went to the door and hummed a line from the night before.

After a moment of silent doubt, he answered with the next bar.

Darcy had arisen early that morning and was horseback by sunrise. He had packed his bag, still undecided about where the day would take him. Just then, the mountains seemed as likely a place as any in which to lose himself. And after that... who knew? However, in case he lacked the motive to go elsewhere, he paid for another night at the inn. It was far from the worst place he had been.

Throughout the morning, he wandered the lower trails, drinking in the crisp air and letting his blood warm. At midday, he took a small repast of bread and cheese. He secured his horse to a tree and hiked some while on foot.

There was one rocky pillar, jutting out over a valley below, and he perched himself on its uttermost edge, his legs swinging freely.

It would be so easy to just... fall.

The moment the thought occurred to him, something recoiled in his spirit. He could never—for one thing, he lacked the courage to push himself from the ledge. Yet, that devilish whim came again and again. The sound of his fingers scraping the rock, his boots taking their last purchase, and his final cry...

Darcy shuddered and pulled back. No, he could never. But that did not mean the hideous thought never whispered to him in the depths, never promised the lie of sweet relief from his sorrows.

Darcy rode back down the mountain that day, and as his horse swayed along the narrow trail, a song kept rippling through his thoughts. Whatever had possessed him—a gentleman of breeding and pride—to spend his night hours humming to a stranger on the other side of the door? Yet, he found his thoughts returning often to that quiet interlude.

Who was that angel next door? For angel she was, he had no doubt of it. Sent to call his spirit back to earth, and his mind back to a moment of rest. If only he had stayed long enough to learn her name, and how long she meant to remain.

Not that anything could come of such a connection. His heart was forever lost to another, but it was that same tug that bound him to Elizabeth, that very thread that seemed to quiver when the woman next door spoke to him.

Her tones were even similar in cadence and expression, and the flippant way she had teased him—egad, he could almost believe it *was* Elizabeth Bennet, in the flesh and staying at some remote inn in the Peaks, but for his sense of reason. After all, he had been seeing her everywhere in his dreams. Why should the madness stop there? Why not hear her in a stranger's kindness, feel her lively wit in the echoes of his darkened room?

For whatever reason, he found himself back in that same room that night. And his heart did give a queer thump when he heard that voice next door—the gentle being sent by heaven to pull him back for one more night of peace. When she greeted him in wordless song, he stepped close to the door and answered her.

For one more night, at least, he had found a friend.

CHAPTER 5

Elizabeth smiled when the stranger's deeper voice replied to hers. "I hope you sleep well tonight, sir," she offered.

That was all she had meant to say. A simple wish for another's wellbeing, and she would leave the room and go to her bed. His hesitation before responding, however, transfixed her there better than any words could have done.

"Sir?"

"I appreciate your concern," came the gentle whisper under the door. "No, I doubt I shall sleep well tonight, but last night's kindness did not go amiss. I wanted to thank you."

Elizabeth silently dragged the rocking chair close to the door and lowered herself to the front edge. "Is something troubling you?"

The man was quiet, then, "It is not something I can speak of."

"Something very dreadful, then," she decided. "I suppose my philosophy would sound terribly flippant in this case."

There was a hint of wry amusement in his murmur. "Your philosophy?"

"Why, yes. Do you not know that all ladies have a philosophy? We have little else to do while we paint tables and embroider cushions but to ponder such things, and so here is my great and profound wisdom. I think on the past only as it gives me pleasure."

"And what if that pleasure is the very thing that recalls the most pain?" he countered.

"Well, I did warn you that you would not like it, but there it is. Perhaps it would be better if we spoke of more mundane matters. Are you traveling for business or pleasure?"

"Neither. And you?"

"I find travel always a pleasure, no matter the distance, when the roads are good."

He was slow to answer. "Yes. Near and far are relative terms, in such a case."

Elizabeth narrowed her eyes. What a... singular response. She cleared her throat. "Er... how long do you intend to remain?"

"I... did not even know I would be returning tonight."

"Ah. So, your plans are not fixed, you are traveling for neither business nor pleasure, and you find even good memories to be painful. I shall infer from these things that you have suffered some tragic blow to your hopes."

"You... would not be wrong, madam."

"I beg your pardon, but you will have to forgive my impertinence. From the sound of your voice, I fear that was a very forward presumption. I would do better to speak of the weather, or the comfort of the rooms, or the excellent food here at the inn."

There was a soft huff of... something. Astonishment,

most likely. "Sir," she asked cautiously, "have I offended again?"

"You mistake me," he answered in a voice that sounded labored. "Your conversation... it is only that the way you speak reminds me very much of someone."

"And... is this 'someone' a person dear to you?"

His words sounded strangled when he replied, "She is."

Elizabeth heard a loud sigh on the other side of the door and felt a deep pang of pity for this man. It was wildly improper for her to be trading condolences with a strange man under an inn door in the middle of the night, but never had she heard such pain in anyone's words. Well... except for one man, last April.

"I am very sorry if my speech recalls someone who is not present," she offered. "I shall endeavor to sound less like this gentle lady and more like a nosy neighbor. Will that serve?"

Was that a groan from the other side of the door? "That... will not, madam. But do not mistake me—I have no objections to your manner of speaking." He was quiet for a few seconds, then in a low voice, added, "On the contrary. I enjoy hearing you... exceedingly."

Elizabeth's eyes widened. It mattered not if this man's tones tickled the neglected corners of her heart. He was a stranger, talking to her in the middle of the night with the sort of intimacy that dear friends seldom embarked upon. She did not even know his name! Oh, what would Mr. and Mrs. Gardiner say?

She ought to go. Bid her best wishes for a restful night, and tell her aunt and uncle about the presumptuous man next door over breakfast. Except... he had asked nothing of her, but from the sound of his voice, he needed everything. So long as she kept her side of the door locked and gave away little of herself, it... well, it ought to be all right.

"I beg your pardon," the man asked abruptly, "but would you be... so kind as to tell me from whence you hail?"

Elizabeth swallowed. "Ah... London. I traveled from London."

❧

Darcy sighed. *London*. Then it could not be Elizabeth whispering to him under that door, but he would have staked his entire fortune on that suspicion. It was not merely her talk of good roads and plotting diverting conversation in the absence of something better to say. It was her voice, the slight catch in her tones he might imagine for laughter, and... well, this was particularly odd, but he could swear that he smelled her perfume.

I truly have gone mad, he decided.

"I believe it is the established custom to reciprocate when one asks such a question," came a decidedly pert query.

He cleared his throat. "Er... London. I come from London, as well. Perhaps we are neighbors."

"I doubt it," she answered lightly. "Will you tell me about your family, sir?"

"There is not much to tell."

"When someone says that very phrase," vowed she, "I am always assured of a long story."

Darcy blinked into the darkness and fumbled for something to say. "I am alone, but it was not always so."

"That much, I had already concluded. You are a very reluctant conversationalist, sir."

"I have been told that before."

"Well, if you dislike the exercise so much, I am perfectly happy to retire."

Darcy's head jerked. "No—please. If you are so inclined, that is. I have also been told that I ought to practice."

She fell dead quiet, and for a moment, Darcy feared that she had slipped away. When she did speak again, there was an odd note of suspicion in her soft tones. "No excellence can be acquired without practice," she agreed.

Darcy stiffened. "Madam, please, I must ask, and I hope you will forgive my presumption. What is your name?"

He could hear her swallow. He had gone too far, and already regretted asking so much. "Gardiner," she replied shakily.

His spirits crashed. How could that *not* be Elizabeth? He sank his head in his hands. Was heaven trying to save him, or torment him?

"Miss Gardiner, it is a pleasure to make your acquaintance," he answered numbly. "I am..." he almost choked on the lie, but it was the name he had given the innkeeper, to keep his presence unobtrusive. It was a name that spoke of new beginning, so perhaps it was not entirely unsuitable. "Adams. William Adams."

"Adams," she repeated. "Is it your custom to make new acquaintances in such an unconventional way?"

"Perhaps I ought to make it so. I believe I have spoken more to you in two evenings than anyone I ever met in a ballroom."

"And now you sound very much like someone I once knew."

"Was he also woefully inept in company?"

Miss Gardiner laughed. "That, he was, but I do not think I could accuse you of such. Though I hardly have the pleasure of your name, I have already spoken with you more than I had spoken to him in a month."

Darcy snorted. "You might not find me so loquacious if the situation were different. I wasted six months trying to find the courage to speak what I wished to... a certain lady. By the time I could bear my own silence no longer, I made such a hash of it—"

He heard a sharp gasp on the other side of the door.

Darcy straightened. "I beg your pardon, Miss Gardiner. It was unpardonable for me to trouble you with these things."

"Ah, no, Mr. Adams," she murmured. "Think nothing of it. Truly. But, I believe I should retire now."

He leaned a hand against the door. He had been hoping she would stay, but she was right to go. "If you are remaining through the morrow," he almost pleaded, "I hope I will have the pleasure of speaking with you again."

There was a hesitation in the next room. "We are staying some days. I wish you a good evening, Mr. Adams."

Darcy mumbled the same and waited until he heard her light steps crossing to the far door before he went to his own bed.

This night, he slept not a wink until dawn, when he fell into a fitful slumber in which Elizabeth Bennet haunted every fleeting dream.

CHAPTER 6

Mrs. Gardiner had felt terribly guilty on Elizabeth's behalf the previous day. Having enticed her niece with promises of rocks and mountains, they had spent the entire day engaged with her own friends. Therefore, she asked her husband to arrange a full day of nothing but outdoor explorations to suit Elizabeth, starting out far earlier in the morning than their norm.

Their carriage was on the road by seven, and a chill mist still rolled up from the valley. Elizabeth pulled her cape a little tighter around her shoulders, but the anticipation of the day made her shiver for a different reason. How long had she ached to explore the Peaks?

And it would be a lie to claim that her interest was all of her own inspiration. Once, when she was staying at Netherfield, she had heard Mr. Darcy praise the majesty of these mountains. The notion had been an annoyance at the time. How dare that man express admiration for the same thing that interested her? But since April, Mr. Darcy's thoughts and words had become her constant companions. What she would give for one moment to make amends!

Mr. Adams next door had recalled so much of Mr. Darcy to her mind that Elizabeth's heart ached. It was her penance, perhaps. Her just reward for all her conceit, for in her way, she was just as guilty as he had ever been.

How bitter it was, that she had wished to avoid the man, and every whisper recalled him! There was within her spirit a tender rip, a wound marked the day she had first read his letter and discovered he own error. Months later, there it remained—larger and more sensitive, and this time, Elizabeth was astute enough to know it for what it was.

She had grown to love the man who first loved her.

The last man in the world, the one who once declared her "tolerable." The same one who had begged for her hand with the gleam of passion in his eyes that she could never, if she lived a full century, forget.

She loved him. And she could not help but wonder if he thought of her with the same regret and longing she held for him.

As for Mr. Adams... if she had any sense at all, she would avoid the sitting room this evening. She ought to go straight to her bed and pretend not to think of the broken voice next door. Had she not seen firsthand how easily her sentiments could be engaged to unwarranted pity?

But there was something... familiar about Mr. Adams. It was almost as if she could assuage her guilt in the way she had treated Mr. Darcy by showing a bit of patience for this poor fellow.

When they returned to the inn that night, Elizabeth had to hasten to her room. Her wanderings over the rocks had induced her to more adventure than her wardrobe could sustain, and she had put a large rip in her skirts. As they had traveled with no maid—Mrs. Gardiner and Elizabeth had been happy to help each other—she would either have to engage a girl from the inn, or mend it herself. She hurried to her room to change while her aunt and uncle took a table downstairs to order dinner.

She pulled off the gown and surveyed the damage in dismay. Not ruined, but she had a long job ahead of her. Perhaps she would be staying up in the better light of the sitting room that evening, after all.

Darcy awoke late that day, astonished at himself for lying abed past nine. He supposed that when one did not sleep until almost dawn, that was to be expected, but not from him.

He took his breakfast in the common room, and it was with some curiosity that he regarded his fellow travelers. What did the effervescent Miss Gardiner look like? Was she half a match for the woman he saw in his imagination? But his imagination would be unfair to any woman, for the only face he could conjure was the one with dark curls and fine eyes, the handsomest face in all his acquaintance.

He lingered over his tea and scone, glancing about with what he hoped was casual interest. Only one woman appeared, and she a harried-looking matron who spent the meal harping on her husband. Darcy shook his head. That was not his Miss Gardiner.

He was embarrassed to confess how long he waited for the lady to come down. Surely, even arising as late as he had, he could not have missed her. By eleven, however, he gave up and went out for a walk.

She had said she would be there some days, and all he desired was one look at her face. Some assurance that he was merely mad, because that was easier than tormenting himself with other ideas. Perhaps he could settle his thoughts by attaching the proper image to the voice on the other side of the door.

He decided against riding the mountains that day. He would not risk missing the lady's party again, so he dawdled in the bookseller's, toured the local chapel, and found a small stream just outside town to admire. On his way back to the inn, early in the evening, he stopped at the ostler's to look in on his horse.

"The left fore shoe is starting, sir," the man informed him. "He's like to throw it if you ride him. I saw it this morning and wondered if you want him re-shod."

Darcy inspected the shoe himself and nodded. "Yes, see it done, please." He drew out some coins for the man and went back to the inn.

The common room was full by the time he arrived. Darcy looked over the heads of the other patrons and saw no raven-haired goddess upon whom to settle his gaze.

"Pardon me," he summoned the innkeeper's wife, "but I was looking for the Gardiner party."

She turned and nodded over her shoulder. "That's him, in the gray coat. Him and the missus."

Darcy looked where she had indicated. The couple were seated at a long table, smiling and exchanging light conversation. "That is... *Mrs.* Gardiner?" he asked.

"Aye, sir, and a good and kind lady. Very generous, sir."

Darcy felt his chest squeeze. So, the woman who had been offering comfort through the door was another man's wife. He watched as the lady sighed in apparent weariness and unconsciously rested a hand over her abdomen. Saw the concern cross her husband's genial features, the way the man urgently asked after her wellbeing and the gentle reassurance with which she answered him. And suddenly, it was all clear.

His new friend was this sweet-faced woman with the honey-colored hair, who was probably restless at night due to a woman's typical indisposition when in the family way.

She was assuredly not Elizabeth.

"Madam," he said to the innkeeper's wife, "I will be dining in my room again this evening."

CHAPTER 7

Elizabeth changed and came out of her room just as a door down the hall clicked closed. That was Mr. Adams' room.

So, he was staying another night. She felt a traitorous flutter at that. Only one man could truly touch her heart, but talking to Mr. Adams in the late hours... it was like finding a friend who never asked anything but her company. She smiled to herself as she tiptoed by his door. Though it was scandalous, shocking, and against all she had ever been taught about maidenly modesty, there were worse ways to pass an hour while she mended her gown than talking to an intelligent gentleman.

And, so it was that after dinner downstairs, she saw to her aunt's comforts and then prepared to settle herself with her sewing beside that locked door. She touched the wood when she heard his footsteps within.

"Good evening, fair sir," she called through the door.

His steps came closer. "Good evening, madam. I trust you are well?"

"Perfectly, I think. Did you pass the day agreeably?"

"I did."

"And did you find what you are looking for?"

She heard a low chuckle. "Just what am I looking for?"

"The answer, of course."

She heard him drawing a stool or chair of some kind up to the door to seat himself. "What answer?"

"What you mean to do with yourself. I suppose that is what you are seeking—a man traveling alone with no perceived destination and sorrows as his only baggage."

"Who said anything about sorrows?" he asked, though his voice was soft rather than challenging.

Elizabeth re-threaded her needle. "Oh, you said that plainly enough yourself. You have many regrets, I can hear, but surely your life is not entirely one of misery. You sound an educated and well-traveled gentleman, and if you have not had some pleasure in life, I am very much mistaken."

"You are not mistaken," he said at length. "In fact, until recent months, I have been... exceedingly blessed."

"In material possessions, experiences, or friends?" she asked as she drew the ripped edges together.

"All of these."

Elizabeth clicked her tongue. "He who has much, has also much to lose."

"I have not lost... all. Only that which was dearest to me."

Elizabeth nodded to herself as she adjusted the dress on her lap. "Then it is not money. No, no, I think I know the sound of a man whose chief complaint is that he has lost someone beloved."

She heard a choking sound. "How have you perceived this?"

Elizabeth looked up, balling her gown in a knot for a moment as she thought. "Because... I know what it is to... regret. I... lost someone once."

Mr. Adams was slow to answer. "How did he die? If I may ask."

"Oh! He is not dead. No, I should have heard that much, but he is gone, just as permanently as if he were. It was all my own foolishness, I am afraid. I do hope... I hope he is well."

"You quarreled?" he guessed. "Or was it something more grievous?"

"I misjudged him," she confessed softly.

She heard him sigh heavily on the far side of the door. "I, too, misjudged someone. Someone dearer to me than life."

Elizabeth felt herself almost tipping out of her chair as she leaned closer to the door. "And have you attempted to make amends?"

"Attempted—yes. Perhaps I confess too much to a stranger and a lady, but... do you mind, madam? I have found few in whom I dared confide, and this, odd as it is, is a comfortable sort of anonymity."

"I do not mind, sir."

He cleared his throat and continued in that hushed, fragile tone. "I have made every effort to... attend her just reproofs. My character was wanting, and I had injured others in my arrogance. These things, I have attempted to rectify."

Elizabeth's rocking chair dipped suddenly when her weight shifted too far forward, and she gave a surprised little yelp as she almost fell to the floor.

"Madam? Is something the matter?" Mr. Adams asked.

"Ahem! Ah... I was just... moving my chair. Sir, if I may ask... of what did this lady accuse you?"

He did not answer.

"Sir, if I ask too personal a question..."

"No, it is not that. Well... perhaps it is. I have told this to no one."

Elizabeth tried to collect herself, settle her bounding pulse as she pushed safely back in the rocking chair. Her hair was nearly standing on end, and her hands were quaking so badly she had dropped her needle. If that man said anything about Kent, or a friend named Bingley, or someone who tried to harm his sister...

But no, Mr. Adams had told her he had no sister. Still, she was nearly ready to demand his name again, and insist that he confess himself to be... someone he could not be. She sighed and retrieved her needle.

"You need not repeat that which is distressing to you," she relented in a softer tone. "Who am I that you should confide in me?"

"Someone kind," was his immediate response. "You cannot know how rare it is that I can speak openly with someone who does not seek some advantage in the moment."

Elizabeth's limbs were quivering. *That tone...* perhaps many gentlemen in the north counties shared that slight inflection, but there was something else in his voice, hushed though it was, that made her lungs squeeze. A cynicism, an impatience, and a desperate yearning for something *different*...

She closed her eyes and clamped her teeth into her lip before she could accuse this man of being Mr. Darcy using an assumed name. It was silly, impossible! It was only vanity inducing her to think thus, and the notion that his regrets echoed so much of hers. She was applying her own tints to the portrait—once again, hearing what she wished instead of the unvarnished truth.

She caught another breath and tried to steady her nerves. "I am happy to listen, sir."

"Thank you," he replied after a moment.

"If I may... might I inquire what else you have done to make your amends?"

"What else can I do? There are a hundred other factors at play."

"Oh, I do not mean for you to confess all to me, but... ah... does the lady know of your improvement in character?"

"Well... no. How should she? I am not the sort of gentleman who would importune someone who has declared a wish never to see me. My intent was more... personal, if you will. I desired to do right, whether she ever knew it or not."

"You must respect this lady's opinions very much."

There was a low groan from the other side of the door. "Madam... she is my guiding star. When the sun sleeps, and all my other cares press on me, it is her light by which I seek to bend my steps."

"And she does not know this?"

She heard his weight shifting in his chair. "I cannot... in all justice... I have other failings to add to all these, with which she is not connected. I could not ask..."

"Is she not a generous person?"

His chair creaked, and she imagined him stiffening to defend his lady. "No one is more so. I do not deserve her regard."

"Mr. Adams..." Elizabeth sighed and rested her head on the back of the chair. Tears were trickling down her cheeks, and she wiped them away. "It sounds to me as if what she deserves is to hear your confession."

Was that a sob from the far side of the door? Surely not... but then, his voice was strangely tight when he spoke again. "But she has no wish..." He trailed off.

Elizabeth tipped forward again. "If I had one chance to

make amends with the... the person I misunderstood, I would move heaven and earth to make it so. But, you see, it is not for the lady to take that first step. She cannot, so you must."

A feverish gasp echoed from the other side. His breathing was labored, but his voice, when he used it again, was lighter than she had ever heard. "Madam... I mean to take your advice. I will go to her tomorrow!"

Elizabeth rose from her chair, her torn gown now entirely forgotten. If only *she* could claim the joy of seeing her Mr. Darcy riding to her! But she had done her good deed—had sent another woman's delight on a path of reunion. "God-speed, Mr. Adams. I will wish you a good night."

CHAPTER 8

Darcy was nearly quaking with excitement when he dressed the next morning. He had not slept a moment all night, but this time, it was not for anguish that he had lain awake. He might... it was not impossible... could it be that Elizabeth would speak to him? Forgive him?

Mrs. Gardiner might have had the right of it. How could she not? A woman so alike in tone and expression to his Elizabeth might also have a similar mind and heart. Well, perhaps that was more fancy on his part than truth, but she did make one very sound point. If Elizabeth *were* disposed kindly toward him, the only way to find out was to ask. Even seeing her face once more, begging for the sympathy he knew she possessed, would be more than he had taught himself to hope.

Others would not be so kind. Others would want to know what had become of him these last months. They would ask about Georgiana. About... about many things, all of which he was ill-prepared to answer. But if Elizabeth would take his hand, hear his pain, all the exposure and fear of condemnation would be worth it.

He was in the saddle just after daybreak, his summer riding coat a poor shield against the morning chill. Soon, the sun would burn off the cool damp, and he would wish for a refreshing drink and a light breeze. For now, he kept his horse's gait to a walk, letting his muscles warm up slowly. Half an hour outside Ferndale, he nudged the bay into a long trot.

And that was when he felt it. A distinct bob in the horse's stride, a pained dip of his head with each step of his left fore. Darcy dismounted at once to inspect the hoof.

There was no rock, no sign of bruising, but one of the fresh shoe nails came out too high on the hoof wall. His stomach sank. There would be no riding even to Pemberley, let alone to Hertfordshire with his horse in such a condition.

Cherington was less than a mile off, though. With any luck, he could leave his horse to be tended, and hire another. Darcy pulled the rein off his horse's neck and commenced a slow, careful amble to the next town.

"Sorry, sir, I've nothing available." The ostler—the only one in town—hardly even sounded apologetic when he refused Darcy's request. "One o' my 'orses is just come in last night, but 'e's done in. Pulled a tendon. T'other three are all reserved, once the fine folk 'ave 'ad their breakfast."

"Surely, there must be something available. I will pay double your usual price," Darcy insisted.

"Nay, sir!" the ostler laughed. "Where would I be if I said to Lord Ralston that 'is 'orse is let out? After 'e's already paid? No, sir."

Darcy sighed. "Well, there must be shopkeeper or... when does the post come?"

The ostler tipped a narrow eye at him. "Fellow like you, takin' the post? You must be desperate."

"It is a matter of the greatest urgency."

The ostler shrugged. "'Round the dinner hour, I should think. Cherington be a small affair, sir."

Darcy grumbled to himself. "Very well. I shall take a private room across the street. Will you have this shoe replaced?"

The ostler grunted and agreed, and Darcy dropped several coins into his palm.

The "inn" in town was little more than a place to fill a tankard. He was able to secure a private sitting room, but he was assured that if he meant to stay the night, all the beds were filled. Darcy was unconcerned at this. Whether he hired another horse or squeezed himself into the mail coach, he had no intention of waiting there. Several hours later, when the post arrived, Darcy's hopes of a quick departure crumbled.

The coach was full, with passengers even crowding the top. Seated inside was a red-faced family with a screaming child, and several young men hung by the rails on the back. None of them disembarked in Cherington. Darcy stepped back before he even drew out his coin for the fare. There was nothing for it but to harass the ostler again.

"How is my horse?" he asked without ceremony.

The ostler looked none too pleased with this interruption—evidence of what a small town this was, for apparently, he could afford to be ill-tempered when it suited him. "'Twere a hot nail, sir," he grumbled. "Set too 'igh in the foot. 'E's better, but not fit for the road."

"And you still have nothing else for hire?"

The ostler shook his head. "Might try Ferndale."

"But I have just come from there! Is there nothing south of here?"

"Sure, ten miles on. Ferndale is only three. You could walk it if you are in the temper for it. What do you mean to do with him?" the ostler asked, tipping his head at Darcy's horse.

Darcy hissed between his teeth. "I suppose I will return to Ferndale and see what is to be had. I may as well take my horse and leave him there."

The ostler shrugged again. "Better walk on foot."

Darcy paid the man, then collected his saddle and set it on his horse. Disappointment crushing him, he turned his steps northward, leading his horse. At least the bay no longer seemed to be in pain from the bad nail, but Darcy would not ask the gelding to carry his weight.

An entire day lost! One of many, to be sure, for had he not been such a fool, he should have set his path for Longbourn months ago. But to have his resolve fixed, and then broken again so quickly, seemed a bitter penance. Surely, however, Elizabeth would still be there a day later. Unless she had caught the eye of some other.

Darcy realized, belatedly, that he was dragging his poor horse by the bridle, trying to forge on at almost a run. As if his return to Ferndale a half minute sooner could bring Elizabeth that much closer! He drew a steadying breath, trying to settle himself.

At least he might once again claim the comfort of a friendly neighbor at the inn, to condole with his frustrations.

CHAPTER 9

"I hope you do not mind leaving a little earlier than we had planned, Lizzy." Mrs. Gardiner was helping Elizabeth style her hair, trying a new coil near the nape of her neck, and she paused to meet Elizabeth's gaze in the mirror.

"No, Aunt, not in the least. I am quite at your leisure on this trip, after all." Elizabeth toyed with a hairpin between her fingers and looked down again.

"I know you wished to see more of the mountains, but we will have another day, surely, with good scenery. It is not as if we must travel in haste, you know. The letter your uncle had from his warehouse was not urgent, but pressing enough that he did not feel it right to delay our return."

Elizabeth nodded faintly in response. "Of course. No, Aunt, if I am reluctant, it was only that I had given Jane this address. There was something I had asked her about... to clarify, and I was hoping to have word from her before we came away."

Mrs. Gardiner lowered herself into a chair with a heavy

sigh. "Of course. And I was hoping to hear how the little ones are faring, but we will see them ourselves soon enough." She puckered her lips and blew out another breath, resting her hand on her middle.

Elizabeth could not help a smile. "May I ask, Aunt, if I am to expect any more cousins one day?"

Mrs. Gardiner's gaze sharpened once more. "Oh, Lizzy, is it that plain? I had not wished to worry you! This trip was about livening your spirits, and this... surprise... ought not to have interfered with your happiness."

She caught her aunt's hand. "What can you mean, 'interfere' with my happiness? Nothing could be more delightful!"

Mrs. Gardiner offered a sympathetic smile. "I only hope I have not slowed you down too much, with needing to rest as often as I have. I fear this trip has not been everything you hoped."

"On the contrary, I have seen majesties I had never dreamed of, spent time with the two dearest people in the world, and made new friends."

"Oh, how could you say that?" Mrs. Gardiner giggled. "Running after my friends' children and taking tea with other ladies three times your age? Lizzy, you are far too generous."

Elizabeth smiled and examined the hairpin again. "Not at all. They were everything charming, but they were hardly the only people I spoke to." She thinned her lips and thought once more of Mr. Adams. His door had been open when she passed by earlier—the room vacant, the man himself probably gone off to seek the woman he loved. It was difficult not to feel a throb of envy for that lucky woman, but if anyone deserved a bit of joy, it was that lonely man on the other side of the door.

Mrs. Gardiner pushed back to her feet—a trifle unsteadily—and patted Elizabeth's shoulder. "Well, you have been a dear, Lizzy. I hope we can do this again next summer, but I fear our years with you may be coming to an end. Someone else will take you away, and then it will be us traveling to visit you at some grand estate."

"Oh, Aunt!" Elizabeth cried. "You are far more optimistic about my prospects than you have a right to be."

"Am I? And I had such hopes that we might stumble into your destiny on our travels!" Mrs. Gardiner chuckled once more, touched Elizabeth's cheek fondly. "We will see, will we not? But, I suppose I ought to look after our trunks. Will you need long to pack, Lizzy?"

Elizabeth shook her head. "No, Aunt. Nothing will keep me here long."

※

It was the middle of the afternoon when Darcy walked back into Ferndale with his horse. His attire was dusty, his feet sore, but at least his horse had not resumed limping. Darcy expressed his displeasure in no uncertain terms to the ostler, who said he would take it up with the blacksmith. And, he promised to care tenderly for the offended hoof.

After ensuring that the horse would be well looked after, Darcy hired another horse for the next day. It was too late to make much of a start today. The business done, he walked back to the inn.

When he arrived, he found Mr. Gardiner speaking to the innkeeper. Darcy held back, watching the latter curiously. He was dressed after the fashion of a businessman. His bearing was mannerly and genteel, his speech intelligent and everything proper. Of course, it would be. Husband to such a fine and gentle creature as Mrs. Gardiner, the man ought to be a worthy fellow.

"You are leaving us, Mr. Gardiner?" the innkeeper was asking.

"I am afraid so. I've had a letter today that begs my return to London. My driver is already harnessing the horses."

"But you will only make Chester by nightfall," the innkeeper protested. "Would it not be better to let Mrs. Gardiner rest?"

Mr. Gardiner smiled agreeably. "It is she for whom I wish to depart. We will be traveling gently, so a few hours today will no doubt serve us better than a longer drive tomorrow. How much do I owe you for the room?"

It was all Darcy could do to keep the dismay from showing on his face. So, he was losing his kind neighbor. He had not accounted for how greatly he had been depending on her sweet encouragement when the dark surrounded him.

A wild thought occurred to him—that of asking this Mr. Gardiner if he had space in his carriage for one more. Indeed, it would answer his needs splendidly. He would even pay for all their rooms along the way, or at least until they passed through Derbyshire again. Such gentle company could only lift his spirits... or cause discomfort to a very agreeable man, who might not think kindly on all Darcy's midnight chats with his wife.

Mr. Gardiner had finished paying the innkeeper and turned around. He dipped his head and smiled when he saw Darcy. "Good day, sir," he said as he passed by.

Darcy turned and watched him go. No... he could not impose himself on the Gardiner party. Much as he would have liked speaking more with that enchanting lady and passing the time with a cheerful couple, he could not ask it of them. A lady in Mrs. Gardiner's condition did not need such discomfort attending her. He would simply have to let her go... one more spot of joy to fade from his existence.

CHAPTER 10

"Aunt?" Elizabeth dropped her book in concern. "Aunt! What is it?"

Mrs. Gardiner had stumbled by the bed and now sat up, clutching the frame. Her eyes were glassy and crossed, her complexion pale and waxen, and she looked dazed.

"Nothing to concern, Lizzy," she panted. "I have had this before—a moment of lightheadedness. It is nothing."

"It does not look like nothing! Let me help you up."

Mrs. Gardiner waved her away. "No, permit me to rest a moment. I think I am finished with the trunk. Just... let me catch my breath."

"You should lie down," Elizabeth insisted.

Her aunt nodded shakily. "Yes... yes, that will be better."

Elizabeth braced an arm around her aunt and helped her into the bed. The moment Mrs. Gardiner lay back, she sighed in relief, her eyes cleared, and her breathing seemed to steady. "There," she sighed. "See, Lizzy, that was all it was. This happened with Emily, too, you know."

"All the same, I am sending for Uncle," Elizabeth declared.

They did not board their carriage that afternoon. Though Mrs. Gardiner insisted that she was well, her husband would hear none of it. The carriage returned to the stable, and Mr. Gardiner ordered a mild supper and tea in bed for his wife. He followed this with threats of sending for an apothecary if he was not satisfied with her color and strength, so the lady bore her husband's care with solicitude and good humor.

Elizabeth, for her part, remained at her aunt's bedside late into the evening, reading to her and keeping her spirits up. She privately agreed with her aunt by this time, that it was only a passing malaise and was not aided by staying abed, but her uncle's worry was not to be denied.

He had sensed his more fretful presence to be somewhat excessive, with Elizabeth tending so gently to Mrs. Gardiner, so he sat in the next room with his pipe and a newspaper. It was not until after ten in the evening that he came back, and Elizabeth retired to her own bedchamber.

She had forgotten that all her clothes were already in her trunk. And her nightgowns, being the least worry for wrinkling, were on the bottom. Elizabeth cast herself over her bed, wondering how badly her gown would look by the morrow if she simply slept in it. Unpardonable! She groaned and sat up again.

It was not her body that was so weary, anyway. It was her spirit, sore and tired after months of affliction. Mr. Adams had awakened the yearning she had hoped to bury, and it was not without some regret that she considered the empty room next door.

How many times had she fancied that it really had been Mr. Darcy? His voice, his inflections, certain turns of phrase... Was it wrong of her to wish that broken soul had truly been him? She would not wish upon him the pain she heard in Mr. Adams' voice, but if she could provide the means of comfort...

Vanity. That was all it was. What girl did not fantasize about mending a man's broken heart? Regardless, she found herself standing at the door of her room, and staring into the sitting room beyond. And then, a glint of metal caught her eye. Elizabeth walked softly in.

It was her sewing needle, dropped again after something Mr. Adams had said the night before. She bent to collect it and stared at its gleam in the candlelight. And that was when she heard it.

From next door, a rich baritone voice was humming.

※

Darcy sat in the chair, gazing at the fire. There were sounds again from the next room, but they were a man's footsteps wandering the floors this night. A cleared throat, a faint aroma of sweet pipe tobacco, and the rustling of a newspaper. Gone was his gentle friend, the faceless voice who might have changed his destiny.

He laced his fingers over his stomach and lost himself to a hundred thoughts. He could not say what time it was when his chin bumped his chest, but he awoke with a start. With a sigh, he ruffled his hair, scrubbed his face, and stood to undress for bed. Unbidden, his throat swelled as he loosed his cravat. The song had persisted in his head the last three days, and he hummed it lightly as he pulled at the knot, then began to unbutton his waistcoat. He fell silent, however, when someone knocked on the adjacent door.

"Mr. Adams?" a familiar voice called. "I thought you had gone."

He smiled and stepped quickly to the door. "I thought

the same of you, madam. I saw Mr. Gardiner downstairs this afternoon, settling his account."

"My aunt was unwell," she replied. "She is better now, but we decided to delay one more day."

Darcy came closer. "Your... your aunt?"

"Yes. She is... I suppose this is indelicate, but she is in an interesting condition, and my uncle is treating her very gently at present."

"Your uncle..." Darcy huffed under his breath. So, this was not the *wife* of Mr. Gardiner, but his niece? A... single young lady? Something tingled in his memory, a flickering recollection just beyond reach, but warm enough to send a ripple down his spine.

"And what of you, sir?" came the voice through the door. "I thought you were in a rush to find someone."

"I... was delayed. My resolve is as fixed as ever—more so, if you would know. Circumstances, however, conspired to keep me here one more night."

"I am sorry on your account," she answered, "but quite selfishly glad on my own. Will you... will you tell me a little more?"

Darcy brushed his fingers against the door, dropped his head on its aging wood, and released a long breath. "Pray, tell me what you would like most to hear."

CHAPTER 11

Elizabeth gasped and almost laughed aloud. How could two men sound so alike? But she would not make light of the ache in his voice, so she schooled her tone when she answered. "Whatever you most care to discuss. Perhaps we may talk of your hopes, as they sound to be on the cusp of satisfaction."

She heard a sliding, shuffling sound, and decided that he had actually seated himself on the floor, with his back against the door. "I pray it is so. I think I could bear all other ills, if she would speak gently to me. Nevertheless, I will not demand it. One word from her would silence me forever."

Elizabeth thought about dragging the rocking chair over, as she had done before, but her uncle had left it on the far side of the room. Well, what matter if she did as Mr. Adams had, and leaned against the door? She bunched her skirts and dropped down, her head resting against the wood that shuddered slightly as their weight from either side shifted it.

"As you are so convinced of the lady's generosity," she

mused, "I will only say that any woman worth pleasing would count it an honor to bestow her affections on a deserving gentleman."

"Worth pleasing..." he sighed. "She is, in every way. If she will find me deserving..."

Elizabeth waited for him to finish that thought, but he did not. She shuffled her feet. "If I may ask, sir," she ventured, "you have mentioned more than once that you had suffered other trials, apart from losing this lady. Would it do your heart good to unburden yourself? I cannot advise you, but I can listen, and you cannot fear that I have anyone to tell."

He was silent, but for what sounded like a sharp inhale.

"Forgive me, sir," she whispered, "I ought not to have asked..."

"It is my sister," he replied in a sudden rush. "She died in April. The very afternoon that I said my last farewell to my beloved, the express came about my sister. She..." His voice broke, and then more cries muffled under his hand. "Forgive me, madam... miss... I shall not—"

Elizabeth turned as if she could see him. "There is nothing to forgive. I am sorry, sir. Very sorry that you should be occasioned such pain."

He sucked in a quavering gasp that echoed in the room beyond. "She was but fifteen years!"

Something in her stomach dropped. A prickle raced over her scalp, and Elizabeth narrowed her eyes. Nausea tore at her—sick dread, coupled with a pulsing recognition. *It could not be...*

Darcy cleared his throat and dug his fingers into his eyes. "It was my fault," he confessed. This, the heaviest grief of all. "Had I been there, I could have stopped it. Had I not been too late, I might have prevented it! And she and my cousin..."

"Your cousin?" the lady asked softly.

Darcy pinched the bridge of his nose and tried to choke back a fresh tide of grief. "He sought to make the reparations that should have fallen to me. He would be alive today, too, if I had only done my duty better."

"Good heavens," whispered she under the door. "And this sorrow—this burden has been yours to bear all alone? Have you told no one?"

"Only that which could not be helped." He clenched his teeth and struggled to reclaim his voice. "No one knows the whole of it—not even my aunt and uncle, who lost their son. I have said more to you than I have to people who have known me all my life."

The lady was silent, for which Darcy was grateful. It granted him precious seconds to catch the cries of anguish threatening to bubble forth. At last, he felt steady enough to make himself heard.

"Madam... miss... whoever you are. I shall forever thank you for your kindness in hearing me. You have pulled a stopper which I fought dearly to keep closed, but I see now that I was only poisoning myself. I dare not say more, but this much... has been a relief."

"But you will say more to the woman you love, will you not?" she asked quietly. "You will confide in her who would keep you and comfort you?"

He nodded numbly against the wood. "I could conceal nothing from her. She is... in fact, you are much like her. Clever and sharp—she dearly loves to laugh—but she is also devoted and gentle. I have seen how tenderly she cares for those she loves. If she will do the same for me..."

He heard her sniffle on the far side of the door and felt a stab of remorse for moving her to tears. "Sir..." she caught a deep breath. "Will you—do you mind—would you tell me this lady's name?"

Darcy swallowed and dropped his head heavily against the door. "Elizabeth." He closed his eyes.

There was a short cry from the opposite side, and the lady was scrambling to her feet. Darcy stood, the hair rising on his neck as he heard the bolts being shot back on the opposite side. Did she mean to open the door? In the middle of the night to a str—

What if she was not a stranger?

His heart in his throat, Darcy cautiously slid back the bolt on his side. The latch turned, and the lady pulled the door open.

And there, in the dim room next to him, with tears pooling in her eyes, was his Elizabeth. She covered her mouth, and her body quaked with a long sob.

"Elizabeth?" he whispered in awe.

She nodded, and more tears tumbled down her cheeks. Then, she fell forward, reaching for him, and pulled his head to her shoulder. Darcy engulfed her tightly in his arms, and let himself go. Her hair was wet with his tears, her fingers softly stroking his face, her slim body quivering in his embrace. And in his ears, a constant, steady refrain. "I am sorry, so, so sorry, my love!"

He pulled back enough to look at her, grazing her cheeks with his thumbs. "Elizabeth! How I dreamed it might be you—I wanted it to be you!"

A weak smile wavered on her lips, and she pulled his hand closer to kiss it. "And every time you spoke, I only saw you."

He drew her under his chin and tightened his arms. "Please, my Elizabeth. Say you will never leave me."

She nodded, and her muffled reply was all his heart required. But then, she turned her cheek against his collar, her fingers still knotted in the fabric over his shoulders, and murmured, "What happened to Miss Darcy?"

CHAPTER 12

"It was last April, the day I gave you that letter."

She had drawn him into the sitting room, urging him to be seated on the sofa near the hearth. He coaxed the cooling coals back to life and then sank wearily down beside her. "You... you read the letter?"

Elizabeth allowed him to take her hand, for he seemed desperate for some reassurance. "A hundred times. In fact, I have it with me even now. It is in my trunk."

He pressed his hand to his eyes. "You kept it? Good heavens. I am heartily ashamed of the things I wrote. My manner alone should have recommended the letter for the fire grate long ago."

"Perhaps, but was my manner any better? Until I read your words, I never knew myself."

His eyes shuttered for a moment, and his jaw shifted as if he meant to retort some bitter recrimination of himself. Instead, he lifted her knuckles to kiss them. "I thought I could sink no lower in my own estimation, but an hour later, I learned otherwise.

"You recall in my letter that I had sent Georgiana to

Ramsgate, where George Wickham followed. I led you to believe that I had arrived only just in time to stop an elopement."

Elizabeth nodded, but a knot was forming in her throat. "Do you mean, you were not in time?"

He heaved deeply. "In time to find her. Not in time to stop what was to come. I took her to Pemberley at once, but it became apparent that she was already with child."

Elizabeth gasped and covered her mouth.

"I would not have given her in marriage to him, even if she had desired it—which, by then, she knew she did not. He meant to force a marriage, of course, to gain her dowry. He cared as little for her as the pounds and pence he would fritter away at the gambling tables.

"I never let him know the full measure of what he had done to her, for if he knew, it would have been far worse for her. We wanted her to have a real chance at happiness, a good future, so we made plans to settle the child in a respectable family. But the babe—a girl—did not survive."

Elizabeth was biting her lips together, the tears standing in her eyes. He brushed her cheek affectionately and continued.

"My trip to Hertfordshire last autumn with Bingley was no more than a ruse. I wanted desperately to remain by her side, to care for her, but her life, as I saw it, would be over if anyone suspected. And so, I sent her away from me, to keep her safe. I laughed and made merry—or tried to—to erase any thought in the minds of others that something might be amiss. But while I put on a smile, Georgiana suffered. Rather than the only family she had staying with her in her darkest time, another stood by her. She was only fifteen!"

Elizabeth stilled and allowed him to brace an arm on the sofa's edge to wipe his eyes again. His chest trembled, and he swallowed several short gasps before he could carry on.

"I sent her with a new companion, Mrs. Annesley, to a cottage not far from Epsom. From there, I could be at her door in a day from Hertfordshire, and even less from London or Kent." His mouth worked, and he rubbed one eye. "Fifty miles of good road, indeed!"

"Ah..." Elizabeth whispered. The reality was sinking closer now. All that time, when he had seemed so barbed and disagreeable, he had truly been in distress for his sister!

"The public story," he continued, "was that she and her companion had gone to Scotland to stay with an aunt of my father's. Richard was the only one who knew the truth."

"Colonel Fitzwilliam?" she asked, in a dread hush.

Darcy nodded, his eyes glassy. "It was he who avenged Georgiana when childbirth took her life."

<hr />

"Do you mean that it was he who challenged Mr. Wickham to a duel?"

Darcy sat up, and Elizabeth's face came into clearer focus as he blinked. "You knew about the duel?"

She knotted her fingers in her lap and looked down. "My sister Lydia is in Brighton, staying as a guest of Colonel Forster and his wife. She wrote the news to Jane, and Jane wrote to me."

"What else was said?" He tried to keep his voice light, gentle, but she looked up at the urgency in his tone.

"Nothing. Nothing yet, that is. All I heard was that there had been an illegal duel. I was sorry that I had not spoken more of Mr. Wickham's character, so others might be warned and... such an incident might have never come to pass."

"You thought this! It is a credit to you, but there was nothing you could have done with such a warning. What you do not know was that I was only two miles away myself when it happened. I had with me a pair of swords, and I meant to ask one of the men of the regiment to serve as my second.

"When I arrived, they were already carrying Wickham off the field with Richard's bullet in his chest. They had fired together... and both hit their mark. There was nothing left for me to do but bend over my cousin as he said his final words. 'Live,' he told me. 'Live for Georgie.' I have been dying every day since."

Elizabeth's cheeks shone with tears. She clasped his elbow, sniffling and dashing at her eyes, and hid her face in his shoulder.

Darcy wrapped his other arm around her and rested his cheek on her soft hair. Could this be real? No dream had ever smelled so familiar, felt so intimate. She was warm, she had weight, and her body shivered in his arms. He pressed his lips to her temple, a final test, and glory be! She was sweet and alive and responsive to his touch.

"Elizabeth," he pleaded quietly, "it is a terrible thing I ask of you, but I will ask it. I have failed so many, broken dreams, shattered hearts, and disappointed myself above all others. But you, I would never fail. I would sell my life to give you a moment of happiness. Do you think it possible—would you teach me to live again?"

She raised her head from his chest, her eyes dancing in sorrow and joy, and traced the edges of his face. "Dear sir, I will have none but you."

She slipped her hand over his jaw, tickling the hair at the back of his head, and then, with the lightest of breaths, touched her lips to his. Darcy forced himself to be still, to allow her to lead him, but when she tugged gently at his lower lip, his resolve vanished.

A soft cry of elation escaped him, and he rolled her shoulders under his chest, tipping her tenderly back on the sofa as he slowly explored her adored face, her mouth, with his lips. He kissed those fine eyes closed and lost himself to the graces of her form. And as the embers cooled in the grate, the night grew, and the last shadows covered them, he could drink deeply of her scent and still sense her light, guiding his heart.

CHAPTER 13

"Aunt, Uncle..." Elizabeth paused at the door of her room as the others were making ready to go down for breakfast. "There is someone you should meet."

Mrs. Gardiner's brows raised. "Since last evening? How very singular, Lizzy."

Elizabeth caught one finger and toyed with it. "Ah... yes. You see, there is another guest on this floor. A gentleman."

Mr. Gardiner nodded. "I have seen him. A quiet, serious-looking fellow. Keeps to himself." He narrowed his eyes. "When could you have spoken to him, Elizabeth?"

She bit her lip. "It is a very long story. I—" She broke off when the door down the hall opened, and all gazes turned that way. Fitzwilliam was closing his door, still looking down at the latch with a hesitant set to his mouth. When his eyes lifted, however, they found Elizabeth, and the features she had once found severe and disapproving melted into something altogether pleasing.

"Aunt, Uncle—" Elizabeth gestured. "May I present Mr. Darcy of Pemberley. Sir—Mr. and Mrs. Gardiner."

Fitzwilliam drew close to her with a smile and bowed to her relations. "Sir, madam, it is an honor."

Her uncle stammered out his pleasure, but Aunt Gardiner—after smiling and greeting the gentleman very kindly—turned a suspicious look on Elizabeth. "What a strange coincidence that you should be staying here at the same time, sir," she said.

"None could be more astonished than I, madam," he replied. Then, with a lingering gaze at Elizabeth, he added — "Or more pleased."

Mr. Gardiner coughed. "Indeed, a remarkable coincidence. How did you discover...?"

Elizabeth flashed a look to Fitzwilliam—one of confident reassurance. He had expressed his concern last night, that her family would disapprove of the manner of their reunion, but Elizabeth knew her aunt and uncle. So long as they carried on honestly, all would be well.

"The truth, Uncle, is that we had been conversing under the sitting-room door. Odd, perhaps, but I think there was nothing improper in it, at least not at first. However, in the course of our conversation, we recognized each other."

Mr. Gardiner tugged at his collar, his features slightly pale. "This happened last night, Elizabeth?"

She cleared her throat. "Yes."

Her aunt and uncle's eyes widened together, and they shared an uncomfortable glance.

"Mr. Gardiner," Fitzwilliam said, stepping up. "As Miss Elizabeth's present guardian, I hoped to ask your blessing on our engagement. I will, of course, tender my request directly to Mr. Bennet, but until such time, I humbly ask permission to join your party and court her."

Her uncle's face regained some of its color, and he emitted a nervous chuckle. "Well, Mr. Darcy, if you put it that way, the pleasure is all mine, and delighted. Come, sir, will you join us at breakfast?"

<hr>

For the first time in months, the sun was shining.

Darcy was seated beside Elizabeth at the table, close enough that he could graze his knuckles over the back of her hand if he chose. And why should he not? It was no innocent happenstance that her skirts pooled deliciously against his leg, or that she had brushed his fingers when he passed her the sugar. The clinging memory of the night before, of finding her tender and warm to his touch, would not be soon forgotten.

Mr. and Mrs. Gardiner sat across from them, and a more humble, amiable pair he had never met. Mr. Gardiner was a respectable, well-informed man—not at all the vulgar, classless individual Darcy had once expected. And Mrs. Gardiner was a merry, kind-hearted soul. It was obvious in a moment that she had her niece's whole esteem, and for good reason.

As for Elizabeth... she was radiant. Her eyes sparkled, her skin glowed with that same dewy softness that once, he had tried so hard not to notice. And her laugh—it was a laugh for the ages, a welling spring of joy and intimacy, of shared delight and invitation. And it was to be his to adore, the rest of his years.

She set her cup aside and gazed up at him, displaying that tiny crease beside her mouth that had caught his notice all those months ago at Netherfield. She arched a brow, as if waiting for him, but he could not fathom why. With a flick of those eyes that held him transfixed, she indicated her uncle, then smoothly made the answer Mr. Gardiner must have been expecting.

"Yes, Uncle," she said, "Mr. Darcy had no other plans in the area. He has indicated his wish to ride with us in the carriage, as his horse is lame."

Darcy straightened. "Indeed, sir. If you can spare the room. And, if you must hasten to London, I would be pleased to collect my own carriage at Pemberley and escort the ladies at a gentler pace."

Mr. Gardiner's face brightened. "Capital! Why, my dear, that would be just the thing." He seemed to beg his wife's agreement, but Mrs. Gardiner was smiling at Elizabeth.

"It seems, Lizzy," she said, "that you will be touring Pemberley on this trip after all."

CHAPTER 14

Elizabeth turned slowly about the sunroom, her eyes dazzled by everything she saw. Even with all the drapes still drawn, and the somber hatchment over the front door to remind her of the house's mourning, Pemberley was... she had no words. If it were left to her to design the perfect house, the perfect grounds, it would look just like this. Her aunt was trailing after her, more slowly, but even she, who had seen the house before, was speechless.

"I never thought to see the private family quarters," she whispered.

Elizabeth nodded mutely. Fitzwilliam had left them in the care of Mrs. Reynolds while he spoke to his steward, and the housekeeper was, even now, watching them with the most peculiar expression. Elizabeth would have expected that the woman responsible for managing such a house would be austere, stern, and terrifyingly efficient. Perhaps the last descriptor was not inaccurate, but Mrs. Reynolds looked far from severe. Rather, she appeared almost motherly, and she was dabbing her eyes frequently and regarding Elizabeth with a watery smile.

"I beg your pardon, Mrs. Reynolds," Elizabeth said at last, "but is anything wrong?"

The housekeeper bobbed a little and made a noise that might have passed for a chuckle, had it not been for the tear she dusted from her cheek. "'Tis nothing, Miss Bennet. Not my place to say, you being the future mistress and all, but..."

Elizabeth came near. "Mrs. Reynolds, I hope I have not made you uneasy by arriving without warning."

Mrs. Reynolds shook her head. "Nay, miss. We were all so sorry for the master, and I will own that I feared something awful for him when he went away this last time. But here he is, back so soon and looking so happy—and he brought you. Bless him! Heaven must have sent you, I declare." She blushed and lifted her shoulders. "Forgive me, miss, I speak out of turn."

Elizabeth took the woman's hand and held it between her own, waiting for the housekeeper to dare meet her eyes. "Mrs. Reynolds, there is nothing to forgive. I assure you, if anyone is blessed, it is myself. Mr. Darcy holds you in the highest esteem, and I hope we shall become dear friends."

Mrs. Reynolds could hardly contain a fresh flood of tears, but she was beaming with pleasure. "Would you like to see your rooms? I've had Sarah freshen them up, and they ought to be ready by now."

Mrs. Reynolds escorted them personally, and Elizabeth noted that every maid, every footman stood a little taller and moved a little more quickly as they passed. No signal came from Mrs. Reynolds, no indication that she doubted those under her. The mark of an efficient manager, indeed. Elizabeth smiled at each person they passed until Mrs.

Reynolds opened the door to an airy, well-appointed chamber. "This one is for you, Mrs. Gardiner. Mr. Darcy said you and Mr. Gardiner preferred only one room?"

Mrs. Gardiner nodded. "Yes, thank you." She turned a soft, admiring gaze about the chamber, but behind all her delight, Elizabeth could read the weariness in her aunt's eyes.

"I think my aunt would like to lie down," she told the housekeeper.

Mrs. Reynolds arranged for a maid to come for Mrs. Gardiner, then she led Elizabeth away. Back down the hall, up a staircase, and around a bend, Elizabeth followed. She was beginning to wonder why she was to be placed so far from her aunt and uncle when Mrs. Reynolds turned around with a guilty smile.

"I have another room made for you tonight, miss, but Mr. Darcy said I might show you this room if you were inclined to see it." Elizabeth arched a brow and peered beyond, as Mrs. Reynolds opened the door. It was the mistress' chamber.

She caught her breath as she cautiously wandered in. The wall hangings, the carpets, even the bed coverings, were all done in soft colors; creams, sky blues, lavenders, and even a shade or two of pink and green. Natural, cheerful colors that looked nothing like the more formal decor in the rest of the house. In fact, it... reminded her more of Longbourn.

"Do you approve?"

Elizabeth jumped at Fitzwilliam's voice behind her. He stood in the doorway, his hands resting on the frame as if uncertain whether he should follow her. Mrs. Reynolds was nowhere to be seen.

Elizabeth turned about once more. "I think there are few who could not approve. Of... all of it," she breathed.

"But this room?" he asked, as he took his first steps in. "I think you will agree that this room is unique in all the house."

She came to him and took his outstretched hand as her gaze still roved the walls. "Quite unlike the others," she agreed, "but, still, it fits."

He drew her close and draped his arms over her hips as he pressed a kiss to her forehead. "I was hoping you would think so. What will you think of my presumption, Elizabeth? I had ordered this room made over last spring, in hopes that someone would bring the breath of life to it again."

She set her hand on his chest and looked up. "You did? You cannot have... you did not do this for me?"

His mouth tightened. "I tried to persuade myself that it was only due time to make it over. The room had not been touched since my mother, after all. I was not intending to propose to you—it was before I left for Kent, in fact, but I *did* know you would be there visiting Mrs. Collins. I suppose..." he laughed self-deprecatingly. "I suppose my heart was already hoping what my head dared not think. Do you like it, Elizabeth?"

She nodded and permitted him to tighten his arms until her head nestled just below his chin. "Very much."

"Good, because this is the first time I have been able to look upon it myself."

She pulled back again. "Why?"

"It was not finished when I left for Kent. By the time I came back, I could not bear..."

"Oh." She raised up to kiss him gently. "I hope you will be able to spend more time here in the future."

His chest rumbled as he kissed her back. "Elizabeth, from now on, this will be my favorite room in the house. You may not be able to make me leave."

"Promises, promises," she whispered between kisses. "I will believe it when I see it."

"Is that a dare?"

"Mmm." She nodded against his lips. "It will be ever so much more pleasant to have you in the same room, rather than propping chairs beside the door."

CHAPTER 15

As Darcy held her, there in the room that would soon be her own, he fought a trembling ache in his breast. How he had yearned for precisely this moment!

Since last winter, if he were to own it, nothing but the dream of her taking her place at his side, coming to make his house a home, had sustained him. Through the anxiety of Georgiana's confinement, in those days when he still knew what hope for the future was, the idea of Elizabeth being the one to put their family back together had given him cause to look forward. There might again be pleasure and merriment in this house, if the right woman came into his heart. Then, when he had lost both the women dearest to him in the course of a day, the mere thought of happiness had been inconceivable.

And now... now, he almost felt guilty.

He had not ceased smiling and, indeed, almost laughing since breakfast the previous day, when Elizabeth had been trading unseen intimacies with him under the table at the inn. With her hand in his, he could bear it all... until he came back to Pemberley, and saw the house still draped for mourning. Then, his passionate denial had to come to an end. Georgiana and Richard would never know this sort of joy.

Elizabeth pulled back from him and studied his face, and it pained him to see her smile fade. "Fitzwilliam?"

He sighed and took her by the hand. "We should go below."

She planted her feet and tugged on his hand. "Not until you confess what has darkened your brow."

"You can probably guess."

"I can, but I would have you speak, you taciturn man."

He laughed wryly. "I doubt I shall ever again have the luxury of clamping my teeth when my thoughts turn to the melancholy."

"No, indeed, and all the better, I say." She caressed the side of his face until he let her hold his gaze, her look everything affectionate and patient. "You are thinking of them," she whispered.

"I could have done more," he answered, in a voice scarcely his own. "I could have sent Georgiana anywhere, or kept her with me last summer, but I wanted—"

"You wanted to give her a chance to enjoy herself without you frowning over her."

"I never... well, I suppose I did scowl a great deal. I only wanted what was best for her. I knew that I tended to refuse her wishes out of hand, even when it was not always necessary to do so, and I wanted to do better."

He sighed. "I was stuck in London on business during the worst time of year to be there. She wanted to go so badly..."

"And you did what an affectionate brother would. You cannot continue to borrow blame that is not yours."

He closed his eyes and dipped his forehead until it

touched hers. "But I left her. After I brought her here, discovered the truth, I sent a fifteen-year-old-girl away to a strange place and with a woman she hardly knew, to endure a process she could not understand."

"Fitzwilliam, did she write to you?"

He blinked. "Every week. Why?"

"And I know you wrote to her, for I witnessed you in the act at Netherfield."

"What does that signify?"

"Did her letters sound as though she cast the blame of her circumstances to you?"

The breath was slow and painful as it left his chest. "No. That may have been the worst of it, Elizabeth. It was herself she despised. She should not have borne it all. Oughtn't I to have done more to protect and comfort her?"

"Perhaps," she conceded. "But short of standing guard over her day and night, what could you do? You could not keep her near you if you desired to protect her future."

He clenched his jaw. "I could have visited her more often. And I could at least have been the one to set matters right. Instead, I failed even in that! Richard—"

"Colonel Fitzwilliam was a man of experience and wisdom. He knew what he was about when he set out to confront Mr. Wickham."

He shook his head. "Richard was in a rage. He was not at all himself when we left Kent that day. He shared Georgiana's guardianship, you know, and had been like an elder brother to her. He was ready to mount a fast horse to Hertfordshire that very day. I tried to talk sense into him, but ultimately what prevailed was that he had an assignment from his regiment. For over two months, I... Elizabeth, I did nothing. I told myself that it would only make matters worse, that even Georgiana's memory would be slandered if I acted then. I could have hunted down Wickham's debts, put him in jail, or challenged him myself, but instead, I came back here like some pathetic sop and kept entirely to myself."

Elizabeth's face was pale, and she rested a hand hesitantly on his shoulder. "There is nothing wrong with grieving, Fitzwilliam."

"There is, when I fail to do what I ought—when others have to take it up!"

She drew a long breath and made him look her in the eyes once more. "What made you go to Brighton at last?"

"Richard. He sent me a message that he was on his way back from the Continent. I had not expected him for some months longer, but I knew what he meant to do when he came back. I was determined to see it done first—who should have done it, but I?"

"If I learned the colonel's character accurately when I met him," she said, "I expect he felt that he was saving you from just such a fate."

Darcy swallowed. "You are not wrong."

"Then you must honor him in this. Do what he asked of you—*live*, Fitzwilliam."

Darcy gazed down at the woman he worshipped—fine eyes flashing, her light form vibrant and intense as she made her demand. And then, with a sob that broke some barrier in his chest, he crushed her to himself, pillowing his cheek in her hair and letting the last of his grief ebb away, as the receding waters of the sea.

"I will, Elizabeth! I will spend whatever days are granted me in loving and holding you. We will build a family, a future, take back more than the grave has stolen. God help me, I mean to live!"

CHAPTER 16

The journey to Hertfordshire was quiet. Mr. Gardiner had gone on with his own coach, traveling farther each day so that he might return more quickly to London. The rest mounted one of the Darcy coaches, with its fine, plush appointments and easy springs, and traveled conservatively.

Elizabeth was disappointed in the four nights it took them to reach Hertfordshire. Not once had she been able to trade endearments under the door with Fitzwilliam, for their rooms were always separated. That was his doing, he claimed. "Do you think that I would be able to leave the door closed, knowing who was on the other side?"

"What harm can there be in talking in the sitting room?" she had teased, though she knew the truth perfectly well.

His face had reddened. "Elizabeth... I fear I might not be able to stop at... talking."

It was delicious watching him fight for equanimity—he, who had ever been calm and rational, and who was presently in great need of something other than the past to tax his thoughts and preoccupations. Elizabeth was more than happy to provide the means of teaching him new patterns of feeling, and employed her powers to best advantage whenever she could. Consequently, by the time she stepped down from the carriage at Longbourn, it was with a smiling and—she could scarcely believe it—*laughing* Fitzwilliam Darcy.

"Lizzy, whatever have you done to Mr. Darcy?" Jane whispered later. "I barely knew him!"

Fitzwilliam was still closeted with her father in the study, and likely would be for some while longer, so Elizabeth coaxed Jane into the dining room for a private word. "Oh, Jane," she gushed, "I can hardly know where to begin!"

Begin, she did, however, and soon, she had related the whole tale in brevity; discovering a lonely gentleman next door, amusing both herself and him with late-night conversation, and then the startling recognition and joy of reunion. There were certain details she did not dare relate even to Jane—especially the particulars of Mr. Darcy's recent mourning and the passionate nature of their first embrace. Nevertheless, Jane was soon in a fair way of comprehending the pertinent details.

"But to find that he loved you still!" Jane sighed. "And such sorrow, losing his only sister and his cousin in such a short time. Oh, Lizzy, I'd no idea that your opinion of him had changed so very much. I hope you did not accept merely out of pity. He is a respectable man, to be sure, and he is rich, but you never—"

"Jane, I must teach you not to listen to my first impressions of people. I was so entirely wrong about him, and never was there anything in my life I regret more than acting upon my assumptions. It has been some while that I heartily repented of those opinions I once expressed, and now, I can safely say that Mr. Darcy is the most excellent man of my acquaintance. I adore him with everything that I am, the whole of my heart."

Jane was blushing by the time Elizabeth finished her avowal. "I think so very highly of Mr. Bingley—more than highly—but I doubt I would have the courage to speak of even him so. You must truly love Mr. Darcy, Lizzy."

Elizabeth grew quiet. "He has a great capacity to love, and to be loved," she mused after a moment. "That was what I overlooked before. There is a depth to him I have only begun to plumb. I nearly missed it!"

"What was it, then, that changed your opinions of him?"

Elizabeth tilted her head with a playful smile. "I believe it was when I first heard his beautiful voice humming me to sleep!"

※

All his life, Darcy had persuaded himself to expect that whatever he spoke for would readily become his. Whatever he desired only demanded the proper price, and he could pay it. This day, sitting in Mr. Bennet's study and begging the hand of that man's favorite child, taught him otherwise.

As the older man sat across from him, his spectacles pushed down on his nose and his arms crossed on the desk, Darcy discarded all the words he had ever expected himself to say in such a scenario. None of them would impress the man he hoped to win for a father-in-law. Mr. Bennet thinned his lips and waited for Darcy to answer his last question.

"Sir... you ask why I believe I will be content with Miss Elizabeth as my wife. To that, I say that I have known what it is to have everything, and I have known what it is to lose it all."

"But you still have your name, your family honor, your estate," Mr. Bennet protested. "What can you mean by this?"

"I have lost the dearest people in my life. How could I account anything else half so precious?"

Mr. Bennet shifted and folded his hands. "Ah, then, you mean to tell me now that you would cherish a wife with equal devotion?"

"No. I mean to tell you I would cherish *Elizabeth* for the rest of my life. Even should you refuse your consent, even if *she* refused me as well, I would love her all my days."

The father scoffed. "Pretty words for the moment, sir. A man's life may be much longer than his attention span. You have no notion of what you speak."

"But I do." Darcy edged forward on his chair and rested his own folded hands on Mr. Bennet's desk. "I have spent these many months loving her. The only reason I had not petitioned you for her hand before was that I believed she would not have me. I have already faced a lifetime without her, and yet my faithfulness was unyielding. I meant, and I still mean, to hold her in the center of my heart, until it should cease to beat."

Mr. Bennet's brows lifted, and his glasses slid down even more. "Well, then, Mr. Darcy, this is a grand scheme you had. And now, what do you propose to do if I give my consent?"

Darcy sat back, and a smile crept over his face. "I have known impossible devotion, and now I know hope. When I marry Elizabeth, I will know what it is to be grateful."

"Grateful?"

Darcy nodded slowly. "Yes. For none of the blessings to fall my way have been by my own hand. I know they can be taken in a moment, so I will revel in them while I can. I will count such blessings daily, and breathe thanks to the one who has given them all. And I will ensure that Elizabeth hears from me, each and every morning, that my sun shall never expire, so long as it rises over her."

Mr. Bennet fell silent. He removed his spectacles and looked toward the window as he blinked and swallowed. "Then, you had better go to her, Mr. Darcy. Tell her I could not refuse her such deep affection as you offer her."

CHAPTER 17

A month later, Fitzwilliam Darcy and Elizabeth Bennet met at the altar, joined by an exultant Charles Bingley and blushing Jane Bennet. It was a ceremony that Mrs. Bennet would long recount in breathless ecstasy to any who could be induced to listen. The church boasted a full complement of well-wishers, and among them were Lord and Lady Matlock.

It had been Elizabeth's insistence, and, after a fortnight of fretting over it, Darcy had seen the wisdom of her advice. He rode to his uncle's townhouse one day to make the miserable confession—Georgiana's indiscretion, its tragic results, and Richard's ill-fated vengeance. After much tearful remorse—and, yes, anger—Darcy left that day with a lighter conscience. And an invitation to bring Elizabeth to tea with the countess. None of it could restore the past, but the future had, at last, been redeemed.

But the morning of their wedding, none of that mattered. There was only the moment the sun broke through the stained glass of the church, its rays blessing hands joined in sacred unity and hearts wholly entwined in the sight of those dearest to them. Mrs. Gardiner wept as openly as Mrs. Bennet, while their husbands looked on the young couples with silent pride. Only Darcy's aunt, Lady Catherine de Bourgh, among all the guests, did not appear pleased, but the fact that she had been prevailed upon to come at all was more than anyone had hoped.

By mid-day, Elizabeth Darcy was mounting a coach for her new home, with a heavily besotted and extravagantly handsome man at her side. "Are you certain you are not too weary to travel?" he asked one last time. "It is not too late to change our plans. We could always turn south to London for the night, even stay some days..."

"And what makes you think I have any aversion to coaching inns?" she asked sweetly.

His face turned red again, a thing Elizabeth had learned to induce with unfailing accuracy. "Well," he huffed as he tugged at his cravat, "I thought perhaps for tonight, you might find it more comfortable—"

She caught his lips between hers, cupping her hand behind his ear and stroking that blushing cheek of his with her thumb. "Do you know what I mean to do tonight?"

His voice was hoarse when he asked, "What?"

She bent his head lower, her breath purposely tickling his skin as she whispered, "Everything. All. Night. Long."

If Fitzwilliam Darcy was red a moment before, now he was positively scarlet. His eyes widened, he visibly tried and failed to swallow, and his hand in hers began to shake. "I..." He cleared his throat, but it availed him little. "I am at your disposal, Mrs. Darcy."

Half an hour, she had said. Only half an hour for her to prepare for bed—and all that word meant—after their private dinner at the inn. It might as well be five minutes for how quickly Darcy's mind was racing. Yet, each time he glanced at his pocket watch, only seconds had passed.

He slowly unwound his cravat and laid it over his chair, his fingers trembling. His waistcoat was next, folded meticulously, and draped with care. For these few more minutes, he would possess himself, center and command all his actions, and school himself with patience. Because the moment he saw Elizabeth, clad in a diaphanous gown with her hair shimmering all around her, all hope of control would be lost.

Only a quarter of an hour had passed, and Darcy forced himself to be seated, to wait for the rest of his life to begin. His heart was in his throat, his eyes might have been dazzled with stars, for all the good they did him. He could make himself think of nothing but…

Soft steps moved in the room next door. An audible swish of fabric, and then, the sweetest voice in all the world began to hum. An angelic melody, the same one that had brought so much feeling and beauty back into his life. Darcy grinned and went to the door between their rooms at once.

"I beg your pardon, madam," he said, "but are you experiencing difficulty sleeping?"

She came immediately to the far side of the door, and he heard her hand resting upon its paneling. "Indeed, I am. I am in need of some amusement. Pray, do you know where I might find it?"

"I am happy to amuse you however you would like. Tell me how I might oblige."

"That is a very generous and unrestrictive offer. You may regret, sir, granting me so much leeway in what I might ask of you."

"I doubt it very much. A lady's wish must be my command."

"Well, I could ask you to sit here in the dark and tell me all sorts of amusing tales," she said from the other side.

"They will not be very amusing, if you are depending on *me* to invent them."

"Then perhaps you will listen patiently whilst I regale you with all the gossip which ladies are supposed to find fascinating."

"I will endeavor to do so, if it pleases you, but I might find it a cure for insomnia."

She laughed. "Then, there is nothing else for it. You must sing me to sleep, sir."

Darcy smiled. "I will, on one condition."

"And that is?"

He gingerly tried the latch, found it unlocked, and eased the door open. There, with the glow of the hearth offsetting her glorious form and her eyes warm for none but him, was Elizabeth. She lifted her chin, still holding herself aloof, and arched a teasing brow.

"My condition is," he answered at last, "that I will only sing while you are in my arms."

Her eyes tipped up as she pretended to consider. "Perfectly shocking. Why, I hardly know you! You are merely the gentleman next door with the delicious voice."

He stepped boldly into the room and wrapped his arms around her. A moment later, after many delirious kisses and much mayhem inflicted to his senses, she panted her mischievous observation. "I declare, sir, your voice is not the only thing that I find delicious."

"No?" He scooped her up, relishing her delighted shriek

of laughter as he carried her haphazardly toward the bed. They tumbled together, all hands and bodies and famished kisses, until the earth stood still, and there was nothing left but soft breathing and tender remembrances of the moment.

Darcy shifted her to his chest, fanning her hair over his bare skin so that he might feel her in every pore, and kissed her temple. Then, he began to softly hum to her. After a moment, she joined him. Their voices blended as their bodies and spirits had, and when the song died away, their breathing was still tied together in gentle sighs.

"I love you, Fitzwilliam," she whispered as sleep began to claim her. "As long as I have words to say it, I will tell you every day how I adore you."

"And I love you, my Elizabeth. As sure as the sun shall never sleep, so will be my heart for you."

The End

ALSO BY ALIX JAMES

Love and Other Machines

Indisposed

Spirited Away

Unintended

BOOKS BY NICOLE CLARKSTON

Pride and Prejudice Variations

Tempted

The Rogue's Widow

Nefarious

London Holiday

These Dreams

The Courtship of Edward Gardiner

Rumours and Recklessness

North and South Variations

Nowhere but North

Northern Rain

No Such Thing as Luck

Anthologies

Rational Creatures

Falling for Mr Thornton

Spanish Translations

Rumores e Imprudencias

Vacaciones en Londres

Italian Translations

Una Vacanza a Londra

Made in the USA
Coppell, TX
30 December 2021